I Am A Dancer

9-99

DATE	ISSUED TO
FEB 1 7 2001	
MAR 1 0 2001	

DEMCO 32-209

Young Dreamers

I Am a
DANCER

AS PHOTOGRAPHED BY
JANE FELDMAN

———————————

To Lena, Kalina, Ayannah, Chamisa, Kelsey, Sarah, Jannelle, Phoebe, Ali,

Haley, and Courtney Rose…the youngest dreamers of my extended family.

They are my most constructive critics and surround me with constant inspiration.

And to the dreamer in us all.

———————————

The Sleeping Beauty choreography by Peter Martins after Petipa.
(*The Garland Dance* choreography by George Balanchine © The George Balanchine Trust.)

George Balanchine's *The Nutcracker*[SM] is a trademark of The George Balanchine Trust.

www.randomhouse.com/kids

Library of Congress Cataloging-in-Publication Data:
Feldman, Jane.
    Young Dreamers. I am a dancer/as photographed by Jane Feldman.
    p. cm.
    Summary: A young girl describes her life and her experiences studying to become a professional ballet dancer.
    ISBN 0-679-88665-6
    1. Lipman, Eva, 1984—Juvenile literature. 2. Lipman, Eva, 1984—Pictorial works—Juvenile literature. 3. Ballerinas—United States—Biography—Juvenile literature. [1. Lipman, Eva, 1984 2. Ballet dancers. 3. Women—biography] I. Title. II. Title: I am a dancer.
    GV1785.l526F45 1999   792.8 092—dc21   [B]   98-33211

Printed in the United States of America 10 9 8 7 6 5 4 3 2 1

There are many people who have helped this dream come to fruition.

I would like to thank Eva, Chen Min, and Ted Lipman for their graciousness and patience in allowing me to document a portion of their lives.

To the New York City Ballet, especially Christopher Ramsey, Rose Ferraro, and Ruth Ann Devitt.

To Holly Hynes and her very gifted design staff.

To the School of American Ballet, especially Madame Nathalie Gleboff, Tom Schoff, Marina Stavitskaya, and Garielle Whittle.

To the Professional Children's School, especially Dania Nauholnyk.

To Sterling & Francine Clark Art Institute in Williamstown, Massachusetts, and especially Martha Asher, for allowing us to photograph our young dreamer with theirs—the beautiful Little Dancer.

To Paul Kolnik, for his performance photographs of *The Sleeping Beauty.*

To the Ballet Company Shop, whose window is featured in this book.

To David Bennett Sterling of the Culture Center for allowing us to use their exhibition of photographs by Linda Vartoogian.

To beautiful Central Park, in particular Strawberry Fields—a constant source of inspiration and joy.

To Vicky Dwight at Chelsea Black & White Custom Lab for years of support and encouragement.

To Kate Klimo, Lisa Banim, Georgia Morrissey, and Gretchen Schuler for their constant support and encouragement and for giving me the opportunity to illustrate this series of books.

To my Citykids Foundation and Darrow School family.

To both my nuclear and extended family—my mom, dad, and Myra, also my sister Jill and her family, and Birdie.

To Kim Zorros, Melvin Estrella, Joanne Golden, Maria and Bill, Lari and Judy, Sandra Burton, Krisha Marcano, Michele McHugh, Margo, Paul, and Jess, and a most special thanks to Helen Shabason for a lifetime of support, both personally and professionally.

To the Creator…source of all creativity.

Hello! My name is Eva and I'm thirteen years old.

My dream is to be a professional dancer someday.

$\mathcal{M}$y mom and I live in New York City,

where I am a student at the School of American Ballet.

We miss my dad a lot. He lives in China most of the time
because he is a diplomat. We try to visit each other as much
as we can. We also e-mail or talk on the phone every day.

y dog, Maya, keeps Dad company. She's a Japanese spaniel. I got her when I was eight and I had the chicken pox. At first I thought she was ugly, but now I think she's really cute.

I've always loved to dance.

My mom was a ballet dancer

and choreographer back

in China, so I started

training very early. I used

to wear a bright red tutu

whenever I watched

performances on TV.

I was three when I saw

my first ballet. It was the

American Ballet Theatre's

Giselle.

Me, age 4, in traditional Chinese dress (except for the shoes!)

Dad and me in Tienanmen Square

That's me at the Great Wall!

I was born in Hong Kong, in the Chinese Year of the Rat. (That means I'm supposed to be charming, ambitious, and picky!) Because of my dad's job, we've lived in many different places:

Taiwan,

China,

Canada,

and the United States.

We like to travel a lot, too. Wherever we visit, we go to the ballet. Dance is an international language!

Me and my parents in Bangkok

I'm the lobster who's smiling!

Mom and me!

started movement classes when I was four. My mom was the teacher. In my very first performance, I was a frog. I don't remember it very well, but I think I had to hop around the stage. Later I was a lobster in *The Little Mermaid*. My mom designed the costumes.

Sometimes Mom and I dance together for fun— aloha!

$\mathcal{W}$e moved to New York three years ago.

It was a hard decision for us, but my parents knew I wanted to study ballet
more than anything in the world.

$\mathcal{I}$ had to audition for the School of American Ballet. My dad drove me
all the way down from Canada for the big day. A Russian lady named
Madame Tumkovsky watched me dance. There was a pianist in the room,
too. Madame is in her nineties, but she still teaches! She had me do some
turns and put my leg up to see how flexible I was. I was so happy when
I was accepted at SAB!

I'm in eighth grade at the Professional Children's School, which is just a few blocks away from SAB. One of the great things about my school is that the students are allowed to pursue their careers during regular class hours. We always have to make up the work, though!

A lot of kids from SAB attend the Professional Children's School. Some of my classmates are actresses, models, and musicians. One of them is even a professional golfer. My favorite subject is English, but I'm best at science.

Ballet class starts at three-thirty, so I have about an hour after school ends to get ready. I usually grab a healthy snack—yogurt is good because it isn't too filling—and put my hair up. Then I change into leotards. At SAB, you can tell a dancer's level by the color of her leotards. I'm an Intermediate, so I wear navy.

Sometimes my friends and I have a few minutes to talk before class. We wrap plenty of Band-Aids and cotton around our feet so we won't get blisters. My feet are kind of a mess from dancing so much.

My first ballet class lasts an hour and a half. We always begin with barre exercises. Our teachers make us spend a lot of time on these basic moves because they're very important in a dancer's training.

Working at the barre warms up your muscles, improves your footwork, and helps you get ready to do jumps and turns. Barre exercises also make your spine stronger and more flexible. There are many different barre exercises. All of them

have French names—such as pliés, tendus, glissés, and battements—because French is the traditional language of ballet.

For the second part of class, we do floor work, which is a lot more fun. Our teachers give us plenty of individual attention. Mostly they tell me to pull up and put in energy, ENERGY, ENERGY! We do the same steps over and over but in different combinations. I like turns the best.

For the next hour, I have pointe class. I first went on pointe, or "toe," when I was ten. Before then, your feet aren't usually developed enough. I started by doing pointe at the barre for about ten minutes at the end of each class. I was very careful to stay on two feet at first. You have to build up slowly to just one foot or you might hurt yourself.

There is no talking during class, but we still find time to have fun. Boys and girls are taught separately at SAB, so we only see boys at performances. Older students can take pas de deux classes, where they learn to dance with partners. Usually the boy is about three inches taller than the girl. That way, when the girl goes on pointe, she won't be taller than her partner!

I'm glad I don't have to walk very far after ballet class because I'm usually pretty tired. My mom and I live in a studio apartment, which has one big living room, a bathroom, and a tiny kitchen. It's kind of crowded because we have a lot of stuff, but it's worth it to be so close to everything. My school is right next door, and SAB and Lincoln Center are only a few blocks away. Also, we have a really cool view from our window!

At night, I have plenty of homework to keep me busy. Sometimes I practice the piano, too. My grandmother Popo taught me to play. She also showed me how to paint.

The best thing
about living in
New York City
is that there's
always so much
to do. On week-
ends, I love to
walk around the
neighborhood,
shop at the street
vendors, and
visit museums.
I go to Central
Park a lot, too.
My very favorite
place to hang out
is the bookstore
near my house.
I can get lost in
there for hours.

So far I've performed with several ballet groups, including the New York City Ballet and the American Ballet Theatre. Roles are usually based on height as well as ability. Every year you grow, so you don't end up dancing the same part over and over. In *Circus Polka*, I was a Blue Girl and an Elephant. I've also been in *The Sleeping Beauty* and *Coppélia*. One of my favorite ballets is *A Midsummer Night's Dream*. I've been in it twice. The first year I was a Wasp and the next I was a Dragonfly. I love the music and the beautiful costumes.

Probably the most famous ballet I've danced in is George Balanchine's *The Nutcracker*. It's a holiday tradition here in New York. Last year I was the Lead Sentry, so I got to wear a big yellow feather in my hat. The other soldiers had red feathers. During one performance, some of the mice waved from backstage and I waved back. That was a big mistake. I dropped the flag I was holding and all of the soldiers piled up behind me!

At least twice a week I take extra ballet classes—with my mom! We rent a room in a rehearsal studio across town and bring our own music. My mom teaches me at the barre first. Then we work on pointe and variations. When we first moved to New York, I was a little behind my classmates at SAB. My mom really helped me catch up.

There's one big difference between my SAB classes and classes with my mom. SAB students can just go home after a tough class. But my mom never lets me forget any of the mistakes I make in *her* class! Sometimes she even wakes me up in the morning with a reminder like: "Eva, your shoulders were too high!" Sometimes she talks to me about stuff like that before I go to bed, too. I don't mind, though. It's not every dancer whose mom can give her extra pointers!

Training seriously as a dancer means a lot of discipline and hard work. This famous statue, called *Little Dancer Aged Fourteen,* was sculpted in the late 1800s by a French artist named Edgar Degas.

Degas is probably best known for his behind-the-scenes paintings of ballerinas, but I like the Little Dancer statue the best.

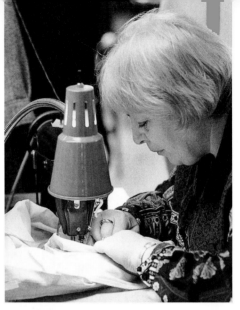

One of my favorite things about performing on stage is that I get to wear beautiful costumes. Holly Hynes is Director of Costumes for the New York City Ballet.

She has a super-talented staff of women, many of them from Russia, who hand-stitch the elaborate trim and beads. This kind of dressmaking is an art that is dying out these days, but I think it makes the costumes look extra-special.

*C*ostumes are stored away every year so they can be used again. If the right-size costume can't be found for a particular dancer, the dressmakers will make her a new one. Ms. Hynes let me try on one of the costumes. It fit me perfectly!

Once I did a photo shoot in Central Park.

A lot of people stopped to watch me having my picture taken. I guess it's kind of unusual to see a ballerina outdoors in full costume! The purple blossoms are wisteria. My grandmother Popo used to paint them because they were her favorite flower. Whenever I see wisteria, I think of her.

$\mathcal{D}$ancers use up loads of ballet shoes every year. Pointe shoes don't last as long as regular shoes. A principal, or lead dancer, may go through two pairs during one performance!

*M*ost dancers, except for the principals, do their own makeup before a performance. I apply more than I normally do so my features will show up under strong stage lighting, but the idea for us kids is to look as natural as possible. There are two main rules: no glitter and absolutely NO red lipstick. That's because red appears black under blue light. Scary, huh?

People ask me whether I get butterflies when I'm performing. I usually don't, but it's easier not to be nervous when I'm dancing in one of the larger ballets. It helps to have a lot of other dancers on stage with me— especially when some of them are world-famous!

Last year I was one of the villagers in the New York City Ballet's *The Sleeping Beauty.* Many of the most popular ballets are based on fairy tales.

My very favorite part of a performance is when the curtain rises and everything comes together: the lights, the costumes, the scenery, the music. My next favorite part is when it's all over and we get to take a bow!

Sometimes I wish I could see into the future. I know for sure that I'd like to dance professionally, but I also want to continue my education. Some ballet kids don't seem to care about school that much, but I think it's very important. Maybe I'll be a poet like my grandfather.

$\mathcal{B}$ut no matter what I decide...

$\mathcal{I}$ want to be the best!

*J*ane Feldman is a professional photographer whose striking work has gained international attention in the field of advertising and for nonprofit organizations that promote youth empowerment. This is Ms. Feldman's first book. She is currently working on her next project in the Young Dreamers series, *I Am a Rider*. A native New Yorker, Ms. Feldman divides her time between Manhattan and the Berkshire Mountains in Massachusetts.